The European Commission and the administration of the Community

by
Richard Hay

Director-General of Personnel and Administration
Commission of the European Communities

Manuscript completed in May 1989

This publication is also available in the following languages:

ES ISBN 92-825-9903-5 La Comisión Europea y la administración de la Comunidad
DA ISBN 92-825-9904-3 EF-Kommissionen og Fællesskabets Administration
DE ISBN 92-825-9905-1 Die EG-Kommission und die Verwaltung der Gemeinschaft
GR ISBN 92-825-9906-X Η Ευρωπαϊκή Επιτροπή και η διοίκηση της κοινότητας
FR ISBN 92-825-9908-6 La Commission européenne et l'administration de la Communauté
IT ISBN 92-825-9909-4 La Commissione e l'amministrazione della Comunità europea
NL ISBN 92-825-9910-8 De Europese Commissie en de administratie van de Gemeenschap
PT ISBN 92-825-9911-6 A Comissão Europeia e a administração da Comunidade

Cataloguing data can be found at the end of this publication

Luxembourg: Office for Official Publications of the European Communities, 1989

ISBN 92-825-9907-8

Catalogue number: CB-NC-89-003-EN-C

Contents

Introduction

What is the 'Brussels bureaucracy'?

There are now not quite 10 000 'Eurocrats' working for the Commission of the European Communities in Brussels, some 2 350 in Luxembourg and 2 600 elsewhere. The other institutions of the Community (the European Parliament, the Council of Ministers and the Economic and Social Committee, the Court of Justice, the Court of Auditors and the European Investment Bank), have a total staff of about 11 100.

Who are these people? How do they work? How do they relate to public servants at national and regional levels in the Member States?

This booklet seeks to reply to the many questions about the European public service, with reference to the European Commission, which is the largest of the Community institutions.

The Community's staff share in the diversity of and are at the service of its 320 million citizens of different languages in 12 Member States and many regions.

And as the Community moves to 1992 and beyond, it is vital that we continue to develop a unique structure of administration, to match the uniqueness of the Community's political aims. We need Europe without Eurocracy.

This booklet also sets out the strategy the Commission is following to this end.

I. The Commission's place with the other Community institutions

The Community was founded in 1952, when the Treaty of Paris established the European Coal and Steel Community. Within eight years of the end of the Second World War, this brought together Belgium, France, the Federal Republic of Germany, Italy, Luxembourg and the Netherlands as Member States in the common management of critical economic sectors, essential for the success of post-war reconstruction.

Over the decades since then, the initial ambition of the Community has been greatly developed. 1958 saw the creation of the Economic and Euratom Communities. Over the following 10 years or so the main policies of the Community laid down in these Treaties were put in place and in particular the agricultural policy.

In 1973 the Community enlarged from six to nine Member States when Denmark, Ireland and the United Kingdom joined. Eight years later, in 1981, Greece became the 10th Member State. And in 1986, Portugal and Spain brought the number to 12.

In line with the enlargement of the Community, its objectives have also been expanding. Today the Community is involved, to a greater or lesser extent, in most areas of political, economic, financial, social and cultural activity. Its tasks include, within the Community itself, achieving and maintaining freedom of establishment, the opening up of public procurement to form the single Community market, technical standards and the harmonization of legislation in a wide variety of fields, scientific and technical research, industrial collaboration, competition policy, agriculture and fisheries and transport policy and, towards the Third World, the external trade policy of the Community and its important contribution to development and aid. In addition it plays a major role in the environment, energy and regional policies, in important areas of social policy and with some areas of education.

The Community has not developed in a vacuum: it has always had to take account of the complex and constantly changing outside world. For this reason, it has relations with most countries in the world, centred on the common commercial policy, for which it has specific responsibilities, and on the Community's policy towards the developing world.

The Community now looks forward to further development, with the ambitious objective of completing the common internal market by 1992 by the abolition by that date of the remaining barriers to free internal trade in goods and services, and at the same time the development of common support policies for the Community's regions with lower levels of economic activity through a doubling of the financial help provided by the Community's structural Funds.

Over the decades, too, the institutional structure of the Community has evolved in line with its growing ambition. The institutional structure of the Community is now as follows:

(i)   The Parliament, composed of 518 directly elected members, constitutes together with the Council the budgetary authority of the Community and also plays an important role in Community legislation and control.

(ii)   The Council of Ministers, made up of government ministers from each of the Member States, is the main decision-making body of the Community.

(iii)   The European Commission is the initiator of Community policies and generally has the sole right to propose Community legislation. It is also the executive arm of Community government, implementing or overseeing the implementation of the policies decided upon.

(iv)   The Court of Justice dealing with disputes concerning Community law.

(v)   The Economic and Social Committee regrouping the social partners and independent members to give advice on proposals in this area, and the European Coal and Steel Community Consultative Committee, doing the same for this sector.

(vi)   The Court of Auditors to examine the regularity and soundness of Community financial management.

(vii)   The European Investment Bank, with a special independent status to act as a borrowing and lending agent for priority investment.

(viii) Three small bodies — the Publications Office, which is the agent for the Community's official publications and serves all the institutions, the Centre for the Development of Vocational Training, and the Foundation for the Improvement of Living and Working Conditions — are attached to the Commission.

The working of these institutions obviously calls for administrative resources, including a budget. This now (1989) is for a total of ECU 2 150 million, which is about 0.053% of Community GDP.

This is only a small part (4.8%) of the total Community budget, which totals about ECU 45 billion — though this large sum represents only 1.1% of GDP and 3.3% of total public spending in the Community. The way the budget is composed gives a broad reflection of Community activity, although many important Community policies (e.g. external trade) do not involve important budget expenditure.

1989 BUDGET BY MAIN AREA OF EXPENDITURE

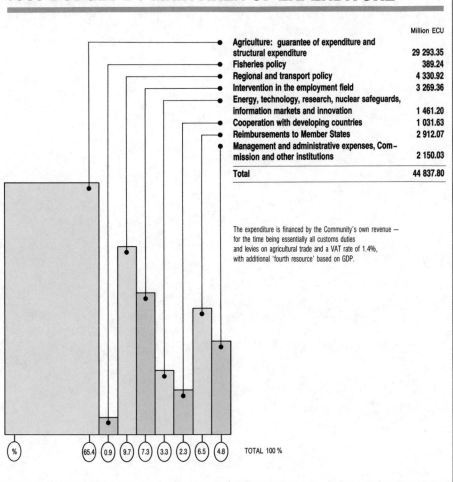

Million ECU

Agriculture: guarantee of expenditure and structural expenditure	29 293.35
Fisheries policy	389.24
Regional and transport policy	4 330.92
Intervention in the employment field	3 269.36
Energy, technology, research, nuclear safeguards, information markets and innovation	1 461.20
Cooperation with developing countries	1 031.63
Reimbursements to Member States	2 912.07
Management and administrative expenses, Commission and other institutions	2 150.03
Total	**44 837.80**

The expenditure is financed by the Community's own revenue —
for the time being essentially all customs duties
and levies on agricultural trade and a VAT rate of 1.4%,
with additional 'fourth resource' based on GDP.

% 65.4 0.9 9.7 7.3 3.3 2.3 6.5 4.8 TOTAL 100 %

II. The European public service: A common framework

The officials and temporary agents who make up the staff of the Community institutions all (excluding the European Bank) form part of the European public service and are employed on the basis of the same set of legal rules. These determine for all staff their rights and obligations, the career structure, the pay scales and the social security and pension arrangements.

The rules were first drawn up in 1962 and were based on the experience of the Coal and Steel Community as well as the then practice of the original Member States. They are regularly amended by the Council of Ministers on proposals from the Commission and after opinion from the European Parliament, and now reflect a wider range of traditions.

The Staff Regulations — and a similar text for staff who do not have permanent status — and related texts cover about 180 pages. Much personnel administration is a matter of legal interpretation. This means that officials can, and do, contest decisions which they consider to be harmful, by formal procedures first within each institution and then, if so wished, before the European Court of Justice (which decided 30 such cases in 1988). A Tribunal of First Instance is being created to handle these and other cases.

The basis of the rules is that the Community needs to have its own permanent public service made up of officials who spend their career in its service. The rules are designed to ensure the quality and independence of Community officials, both at the moment of their recruitment and thereafter in the course of their careers. This is a fundamental option, for it would have been possible for the Community to be serviced by temporary staff serving for short periods and mainly drawn from national administrations. This option was set aside in favour of the same sort of structure as exists in most of the Member States for their own public service, and for the same reasons — the need to guarantee independence in the face of the pressures which exist in public administration.

The rules therefore require that recruitment be conducted in as objective a manner as possible. No discrimination is allowed on the basis of race, sex or creed. Entry is by means of competition (almost always involving both written and oral tests) open equally to nationals of every Member State.

At present, competitions are mainly organized by each institution separately, but sometimes two or more institutions act together. Discussions are now taking place to try to move towards systematic interinstitutional recruitment, which would enable us to come to the recruitment market in a more concentrated and effective way.

Once appointed, each official accepts the obligation to carry out his or her duties with only the interest of the Community in mind.

A common career structure is laid down, with four categories of staff corresponding to the minimum educational qualifications required for entry to each category:

D category — primary education certificate;
C category — secondary educational qualifications;
B category — university entrance level qualifications;
A (and LA for linguistic staff) category — university degree.

Each category is divided into grades, corresponding to different levels of responsibility (see Annex 1). The basic management structure is that of a *unité* headed by an A3, A4 or sometimes even A5, official. Staff are grouped into these units, in accordance with their different tasks and responsibilities. The head of unit will usually be under the authority of a director (A2) who in turn will normally report to a director-general (A1) who represents the highest level that an official may reach in each institution.

In turn, each grade is divided into a limited number of salary steps over which advancement takes place every two years. Officials may be promoted from one grade to the next, after a minimum period in each grade. By competition officials may also move to a higher category; a significant number of officials do this.

Pay scales for all Community servants are decided by the Member States meeting in the Council of Ministers. The rules lay down that pay should be reviewed at least annually, and that levels should be adjusted (up or down) in accordance with movements in the levels of pay of national public servants. Each official of the same grade and seniority is paid the same at each place of work, while arrangements are made to ensure that pay has the same purchasing power in different places of work. Pay is subject to tax (with a maximum rate of 45%), of which the proceeds are paid directly into the Community budget (any other income a Community official may have is subject to national taxation in the country from which he or she was recruited. Taxation levels have not been reviewed in recent years but increases in national taxation rates have been included before calculating salary changes for Community staff. There is however an additional 'crisis levy' (an additional temporary tax, introduced in July 1981, to contribute towards the costs of the economic crisis) which is deducted from salaries at a variable level which for most senior staff is now 7.62%. Some allowances are also paid, and other deductions made (see Annex 2).

To illustrate pay levels, two examples are given of basic monthly salaries (as at 1.1.1989):

(i) a university graduate in mid-career (at least 10 years' experience) would receive BFR 182 499;

(ii) a secretary also in mid-career (between 12 and 15 years' experience) would receive BFR 86 555;

(more details are given in Annex 1).

When the Community began, the Member States decided to start with relatively high salaries in order to attract high-quality staff from the private as well as the public sectors to the new institutions. This starting point, and the same need, still influences Community pay, but the differences with national public service salaries have been reduced over the years, particularly at senior levels. It is also necessary to take account of the often higher levels of pay paid by other international or diplomatic employers in the private as well as the public sectors, since these concern the same population of people who are prepared to leave their country to take up employment. Increasingly, too, candidates are influenced by the fact that in their home country both they and their partners work, which is often much more difficult, at the Community's places of work.

The Community also has its own pension system, which is based on the contributory principle.

Finally, the Community has established its own sickness insurance system, which works on the same basis as a national sickness insurance scheme as found in many Member States.

III. The Commission's organization

As we have seen, each Community institution has its own role to play and therefore has its own structures, staffing patterns and management problems.

Because it has been given the broadest responsibilities, the Commission is by far the largest of the Community institutions. This booklet deals with the Commission's structures and staff.

As the initiator of Community policy, the Commission alone is responsible for presenting draft Community legislation to the Council. The Commission is also the executive arm

The Berlaymont building, at the Schuman roundabout in Brussels, headquarters of the European Commission.

of the Community. Over the last 35 years many tasks have been entrusted to it either directly by the Treaties or by the Council of Ministers.

The role of guardian of the Community Treaties also falls to the Commission, to ensure that they and the other legal instruments adopted by the Community are complied with. If they are not, it is for the Commission to take action and, if necessary, bring proceedings before the Court of Justice.

The Commission has therefore to be exponent and protector of the Community interest in all circumstances. It must first identify this interest and support it against the often very disparate national interests. It must then ensure that it survives the often difficult negotiations in the Council, and must finally carry it into the implementation of policies once decided.

The political level: the Commissioners

The responsibility for carrying out these many tasks falls on the College of the Commission, the body of now 17 Commissioners coming from each of the Member States. The College is headed by a President, and at present there are six Vice-Presidents. It takes its decisions collegiately, and for this purpose meets at least one day each week.

Each Commissioner has a personal staff, called a cabinet, which works directly with him and which helps him prepare his contribution to the work of the College, and his contacts with the services, with the other institutions, with the Member States and with the general public.

Each Member of the Commission has special responsibility for some part of the institution's work, and for the services dealing with these areas of responsibility.

Policy and executive services

The largest policy unit is agriculture, because of the extent of the Community's agricultural policy and its direct impact on the working life of the Community's 8 million agricultural workers. Fisheries became a separate service as the Community's policy in this area developed.

External relations and development both reflect very well-established Community policies, in the field of commercial relations on behalf of the 12 Member States in negotiations with the USA, Japan and indeed all other trading partners, and in administering the Community's ever-growing programme of aid to developing countries both linked to the Community by the Lomé Agreement and the non-associated countries. The Community's competence for external trade is reflected in the need for a service dealing specifically with customs matters such as tariffs and import arrangements.

The Commission has more than 90 delegations or sub-delegations around the world, to provide permanent representation in most of those countries or areas for which the policies of the European Community are significant, and also for international organizations of which it is either a full member or observer. In particular, the Commission is represented in 62 of the 66 States in Africa, the Caribbean or the Pacific with which the European Community has special relations.

A large group of services deal with different aspects of the economic activity of the Community. The Economic and Monetary Directorate-General provides the essential analysis and direction. Industry, competition, social affairs and transport are also amongst the oldest of the services of the Commission, but they have been joined over the years by services dealing specifically with tax and financial institutions, energy, with new technologies and with small and medium-sized enterprises, and lately by services dealing with political priorities like consumer policies and youth and education. The Euratom Supply Agency is responsible for the tasks laid down in the Euratom Treaty for supply of peaceful nuclear material, while inspection is carried out by a service of the Energy Directorate-General. The Community's general role in research, beyond the activities it carries out itself or directly organizes elsewhere which are briefly described below, is exercised by the Research Directorate-General and (for the publication of research results) by the New Technologies Directorate-General.

President Delors has said that a Commission official has six professions:

(i) to innovate, as the needs of the Community change;

(ii) to be a law maker, preparing the legal texts needed for Community decisions;

(iii) to manage the growing number of Community policies;

(iv) to control respect for Community decisions at all levels;

(v) to negotiate constantly with all the different actors in the Community process;

(vi) to be a diplomat in order to be successful in the five other professions.

Structural policy, and the accompanying Funds (Regional, Social and Agricultural) are managed by the Directorates-General for Regional Policy, Social Affairs and Agriculture. Necessary coordination is provided by a small separate service. The Community's borrowing and lending activity is undertaken (other than by the European Investment Bank) by the Credit and Investments Directorate-General (lending to the coal and steel industries).

Research

The logic of the benefits of common effort in the research field as well as in other areas was recognized from the outset of the Communities. At first, it was confined to coal and steel and to the peaceful use of atomic energy (under the ECSC and Euratom Treaties), but over the decades this activity too has diversified and expanded. It now tends to take one of three forms.

First, we have the Community's own research. This is mainly conducted at the Joint Research Centre (JRC). The JRC is made up of four sites located at Ispra (Italy), Karlsruhe (Germany), Petten (Netherlands), and Geel (Belgium). At the outset based on research into nuclear fission, the JRC's activities have steadily expanded: in the nuclear field they concentrate on safety research, and now include many non-nuclear activities including the environment, norms and standards, materials research, and remote sensing from satellite.

The Joint Research Centre is organized by specialized institutes, dealing with:

(i)   Central Bureau for Nuclear Measurements (Geel).

(ii)   Institute for Transuranium Elements (Karlsruhe).

(iii)   Institute for Advanced Materials (Petten — Ispra).

(iv)   Institute for Systems Engineering (Ispra).

(v)   Institute for the Environment (Ispra).

(vi)   Institute for Remote Sensing Applications (Ispra).

(vii)   Institute for Safety Technology (Ispra).

(viii) Centre for Information Technologies and Electronics (Ispra).

(ix)   Institute for Prospective Technological Studies.

Second, the Community is also a partner in the JET Joint Undertaking in the field of controlled nuclear fusion. The JET or Joint European Torus — a huge experimental fusion device — is located in Culham (United Kingdom).

Third is 'shared-cost research'. This is carried out on the basis of Community programmes in European research institutes and universities and in industry, with financial aid from the Community budget. It requires central coordination and in some cases direction. This area has been the fastest growing in recent years, particularly in the field of new technologies. Major programmes such as Esprit, Brite and RACE have gained much support from Member State governments and industry and have made significant progress in the areas of informatics and telecommunications.

Aerial view of the Community's Joint Research Centre in Ispra, North Italy.

By the nature of these different activities, the first involves the most Community staff. There are some 2 180 staff in the JRC, and 190 Community staff involved in the JET project. About 700 staff are involved in the shared-cost activities, of whom two-thirds are now working in the area of new technologies. This staff, scientists or engineers by training and many of them from university laboratories or industrial research centres, are actively involved in the implementation of these programmes. Their central position means that they play a vital role in the dissemination of the ideas and knowledge which they are instrumental in developing.

Coordination and support

There are also services which provide essential support to these activities, and more widely. The Secretariat-General is responsible for policy coordination of all the different activities of the institution, prepares the Commission's decision-taking and is responsible for relations with the Council and the Parliament. The Statistical Office, which works closely with the national statistical offices, produces Community statistics in many areas which are used very widely throughout the Community and indeed the world. The Legal Service and the Budget Directorate-General are important both internally and towards the other Community institutions.

The Spokesman's Group and the Information Directorate-General are vital for contact with the press and the wider public. To help in this, several of these services have also taken on new activities as the Community's role expands — for example, for culture and the European passport.

To provide points of constant contact and information for people and organizations in each country, the Commission has offices in each of the 12 Member States. In several of these States there are also sub-offices in some major towns or regions. As with the delegations in countries outside the Community the key members of the staff are Commission officials, and the rest — a majority — are locally employed staff.

Finally, there are some services which are primarily important for internal management: financial control, security and personnel and administration. This latter is a very large unit, because it supplies all the infrastructure services to the Commission — informatics support, internal mail, transport, staff canteens, library, buildings — as well as being responsible for personnel policy and procedures including recruitment and training and for running the Community's own social security scheme.

Language

The integration of Europe can only work with the agreement and willing cooperation of Member State governments, of the social partners and of the European citizens. Everything the European Community does — and especially its legislation which is directly applicable — must be able to be understood by people in the 12 Member States. It is not compatible with the ideal of the Community that individual languages should disappear. On the contrary, the richness of the Community requires that they should exist and develop. Yet it is vital that languages should not be a barrier to the Community's common effort. This means that those who come together to work in the framework of the Community must be helped to be able to understand each other as they talk, while documents intended for the other European institutions, the Member States, the social partners and the general public must be available in the nine official languages of the Community (Danish, Dutch, English, French, German, Greek, Italian, Portuguese and Spanish).

There are 72 different possible pairs of official languages of the Community.

A meeting with simultaneous interpretation at the European Commission. Every participant from every Member State must be able to speak in his or her own language.

This applies in particular to Community legislation. As the Community is part of the government which affects each Community citizen, it is essential that its laws (regulations, directives, etc.) are available in all nine official languages during the procedures for their adoption. And as they are applicable throughout the European Community, they have to be published simultaneously in the nine official Community languages in the *Official Journal of the European Communities.*

The aim of the translation service is therefore not only to translate texts into up to eight other languages but also to ensure that the end result looks like the original texts. The ideal is that everyone in the European Community should be able to read a Community text and fully understand it, thinking that it was written in his or her own language.

The difficulty of achieving this aim is great when confronted by the mass of work — in 1988, the Commission translated about 900 000 pages — but also by the technicality of much of the work. The service therefore maintains a large terminology section, which from time to time publishes multilingual vocabularies in different areas of expertise so that the benefits of the Commission's knowledge may be made available to others. The Commission is also working on computer-assisted automatic translation.

Similarly, the Commission's Joint Interpretation and Conference service provides interpreters at all meetings attended by representatives of Member State governments or specialist interest groups and at many other meetings each week. It also supplies interpreters for meetings of the Commission and of Commission bodies (committees, etc.) involving people from Member States, and of the other Brussels-based European institutions (the Council of Ministers and the Economic and Social Committee) and of the European Investment Bank in Luxembourg.

Interpretation is provided according to need at the many hundreds of meetings held every week with participants from some or all of the 12 Member States. In some cases it is not necessary — such as meetings attended only by multilingual diplomats — and in others interpretation only from and into some Community languages is all that is required.

The requirements for interpretation vary widely, and when necessary, the service calls on freelance interpreters to complement its own staff, as also does the translation service.

To cope with the tasks the Commissions has a large language staff. With more than 460 interpreters and 1 200 translators, over 25% of university graduates employed by the Commission are directly engaged on language work. In the smaller Community institutions this figure can be as high as 70% of graduates. In addition, the Commission's language services have a large supporting staff — 650 people performing functions like typing the different language versions of each document, providing technical support for meetings, and carrying out the normal supporting tasks of any administration. This total of 2 200 staff seriously underestimates the total of those engaged on language work because in all the services many officials undertake some translation and much typing of different language versions of texts. A rough estimate is that this adds at least another 500 people's work each year to bring the total effort due to language to at least 2 700.

Publications Office

It is not enough to legislate and to translate; the authorities and the public have to be able to have access to the proposals and decisions of the Community institutions, and also to the wide range of information that is collected at Community level. This is the task of the Publications Office of the European Communities. This body which was founded in 1969 is at the service of all the Community bodies, and is managed by an interinstitutional committee although it is administratively attached to the Commission.

The Office is the only publisher in the world to produce systematically in nine languages, which means that it is amongst the largest publishing houses in the world. Forty periodicals and some 900 other publications are issued each year and reach 500 000 subscribers and users in the Community and world-wide. The Official Journal appears daily in at least three editions, each in nine languages, which is an enormous technical and managerial task.

Modernization of the means of publishing is leading to archives on optical disk able to retain on a small space very large quantities of texts and pictures. These are now available to users either on paper, on screen or by telecopy. This is only one new development to enable the Office to keep up with the increasing activity of the Community.

Location of the Commission's departments

These activities are not undertaken in the same place, but are to be found in different parts of the Community and beyond. The Commission's headquarters are in Brussels and Luxembourg, and the majority of its staff are there. But its research staff is spread over five Commission centres throughout the Community with smaller numbers of staff attached also to some national centres, while there are the Press and Information Offices in each Member State and the external delegations.

Commission staff by location (1.1.1989)	
Brussels	9 854
Luxembourg	2 349
Ispra (Joint Research Centre)	1 587
Other research centres	528
Press and Information Offices in the Community	157
Delegations outside the Community (incl. ACP, etc.)	414
Other	49
Total	14 938

IV. Characteristics of the Commission as a public service

A young organization

The first characteristic of the Commission, in contrast with most national public services, is that the Commission, like the other Community institutions, is young and has been subject to many changes. The Commission traces its origins to the High Authority of the European Coal and Steel Community, set up in 1952. In 1958 the European Economic and European Atomic Energy (Euratom) Communities were established, each with its own separate Commission. It was not until 1967 that these three bodies were merged into one organization, known as the European Commission or Commission of the European Communities.

Within five years of this merger came the first enlargement of the European Community, to include Denmark, Ireland and the United Kingdom. With it came the need to absorb a large number of staff of these nationalities. In 1981 there was a second enlargement, with the accession of Greece. And in 1986 the European Community was further enlarged to include Spain and Portugal.

The Community has gained by these enlargements. But each has meant a readjustment of the Commission's staffing and organization. At the fusion of the executives in July 1967 and on enlargement some staff have been invited to leave to make way at least in part for new Member State officials. And on each occasion and indeed frequently in the appointment of a new Commission covering four years, there has been some adaptation of internal organizational structures.

In comparison with much larger national public services with decades and even centuries of experience behind them, the Commission thus has the possibility of great flexibility in its organization which has not become rigid. This is an asset which is exploited as the political objectives of the Community evolve. This flexibility has to be balanced with the need that any organization has for continuity and stability, and for steps to help manage careers made rather uncertain by an uneven (if improving) age structure.

Work content

A second characteristic of the Commission is that, in contrast to the national administrations, it has very little direct management of policies concerning the individual firm or citizen. The Community of course does directly affect individuals or firms. But, in general, it does so through policies which are applied or administered by the Member States at national level within a legal framework decided at Community level and sometimes with funds provided from the Community budget and controlled by the Community. A far greater proportion of work than in a national administration is devoted in the Commission to development of new policies.

In this context, however, it is important to note that under the Community system of institutional checks and balances, the Commission proposes and executes, but only rarely legislates.

It does not have the same relationship with the legislative process of the Community as does a Member State government with its country's legislature where normally the national government represents the majority. Once adopted by the Commission, the proposal:

(i) goes to the Parliament for an opinion, prepared by a specialist committee;
(ii) goes to the Economic and Social Committee for an opinion, also prepared by a committee;
(iii) is examined by national officials who help prepare a decision which is finally examined by the relevant national ministers meeting together in the appropriate Council.

In management terms, different consequences flow from this. Initiatives of the Commission take a long time to be decided, which can be very frustrating for the official who has prepared the proposal and developed expertise and contacts in the area. More important, the result is that each A-category official is in practice called on not only to develop but also to promote ideas. The Commission is surrounded by pressure groups, and any proposal which the Commission wishes to get decided needs to be explained to the appropriate groups in the hope that these will in turn help to mobilize public opinion and so encourage the national authorities to agree to the Commission's ideas. In addition, officials are regularly called on to explain and defend proposals before committees of the European Parliament, the Economic and Social Committee and the Council of Ministers. The process sometimes takes years.

Multinational staff

A third characteristic is that the Commission is staffed with a mixture of nationalities. This is a source of immense richness in daily contacts and longer-lasting friendships. But it carries with it certain constraints. Language is one. While within the Commission there is hardly ever recourse to translation or interpretation, the fact that most people are working in a language other than their own undoubtedly makes it more difficult to communicate. Language is the expression of a culture; national thought processes are not identical. So meetings take longer, and more effort is required to understand, and to cope with situations in which misunderstandings come to light.

In addition, cultural differences affect management styles. Many officials feel some inhibition about exercising management in as direct a way as they would do in a single culture situation, because they are not certain that their colleagues of different nationalities share an identical approach to questions of authority, discipline and so forth.

On top of the stresses and strains that these factors produce in everyday life, there is a further phenomenon which affects particularly senior staff. In the Commission, it is recognized that there is a political need to try to maintain a certain balance in the presence of different nationalities in top management posts. At the B, C and D levels, the only factor which influences the choice of candidate is the interest of the service. At the level of Directors-General, on the other hand, the Commission seeks to maintain a careful balance between nationalities, and this balance is also maintained — but with increasing flexibility — at the levels of director and head of unit, at which level the flexibility is now substantial. This political need is seen as affecting the careers of some officials and can produce some frustration.

Dependence on outside expertise

As already mentioned, the European Commission is a small organization, seen in the light of the range of tasks it undertakes. This means that, since the Community deals with many very specialized matters, the Commission is heavily dependent on outside expertise.

In part the Commission seeks to bring in this expertise temporarily. As well as the schemes for bringing in national officials for short periods, the Commission also concludes many contracts with outside private sector consultants or experts. In addition, it is constantly in touch with officials and others in each of the Member States to help it draw up proposals or administer existing policies. Each week there are about 150 meetings with outside experts, which are vital for the Commission to make up for its lack of internal expertise. Officials also need to travel a lot to the Member States for the same reasons.

When the Commission wanted to prepare a directive on machine safety standards, the DG responsible:

(i) sent a questionnaire to all the Member States;

(ii) produced a working paper based on the results;

(iii) set up a working party with representatives of the Member States' institutions concerned, and also the relevant European employers and union organizations;

(iv) consulted the other directorates-general with an interest;

(v) only then finalized a draft proposal.

This practice is very valuable; it extends the involvement in the Community enterprise very widely amongst those concerned in Member States. And it is good to have experience of and contact between national and Community public services.

In management terms it is interesting to note that the normal hierarchy is in practice significantly shortened because at any one time some officials in the hierarchy will be away on business trips or in all-day meetings. It is only slightly a caricature to say that any particular topic is only well-known to two officials — a junior official who knows it all and a senior official who gives policy guidance, and has high-level contacts. This can encourage a tendency to identify with a subject, and can also make it objectively harder to achieve staff mobility because knowledge of a subject is concentrated on an individual. It also favours the separation of grade and function mentioned above.

The multinational character of the Community cannot be limited to presence of different nationalities within the Commission's services or to the many meetings on specific topics already mentioned. There is a need for contacts of very many kinds. One is for the presence of Commission officials in the different Member States, to talk to government departments, to industry, to the public, in order both to explain and to learn personally the situation in a country which perhaps they do not know very well.

Another is to bring those concerned in the Member States to the Commission. Many groups of visitors are received each year. In addition, each year two groups of about 250 trainees are selected from amongst young university graduates, mainly from the Member States but also including some from other countries, who spend five months learning about the Community and about the Commission.

Continuing in the same direction, the Commission has also developed a scheme by which national civil servants, from central, regional or even local administrations, may be detached by their employers (who continue to pay their salary) to work in the Commission for periods of up to three years, so that they may both contribute to the Community's construction and also learn about the Community so as to be able to apply this knowledge in their later career. This scheme (which can also in some circumstances include people from the private or nationalized sectors) has been welcomed by the Member States, and should surely continue in the future as the contacts between the Community and national levels of administration deepen. In addition, some national officials are recruited for slightly longer periods as temporary officials, but with the same idea that they should then return to their parent administration to apply at that level the expertise they have gained.

At 1.1.1989, there were 203 national officials working in the Commission on detachment:

B	= 11	E	= 10	L	= 0
DK	= 13	F	= 46	NL	= 13
D	= 22	IRL	= 18	P	= 8
GR	= 33	I	= 10	UK	= 19

At the same date there were 35 Commission officials on detachment to national or regional administrations.

Openness of administration

If the Commission is open to the outside, it is naturally also open internally. The multicultural nature of the European civil service has led to rules which give a large consultative role to elected staff representatives. These have a part to play in recruitment and all but the most senior promotions, as well as in many other areas of staff policy and in such matters as security and health at work. This participation, now also reflected in the presence of staff unions (with the right to strike, fortunately rarely exercised) with whom the Commission has concluded an agreement laying down the rights and duties of both the unions and the administration in the negotiation of matters that cannot be handled by the elected staff representatives, although of course at the end of the day it is the Commission that takes final decisions.

In addition, the Commission has created the job of mediator to meet the needs of some individual members of its staff. The mediator acts as intercessor between the administration and its officials, and has the task of looking into any problem or difficulty officials encounter in their professional life, in their working conditions and in their relations with their superiors and the administration, when officials ask for this.

The mediator is completely independent and deals objectively with every case. Officials seeking advice or wishing to pursue complaints may have access in confidence at any time. The mediator maintains an open door policy in Brussels and pays regular visits to Luxembourg and the Community research centres in order to be available to officials in the main places of the Commission's work.

Most complaints come from lack of information, or from misunderstandings caused by different national working habits, cultures and expectations. The mediator has direct access to all the Commission's services, and he either advises the official or if need be may intervene directly in the official's service or directorate-general to help sort out problems.

Management techniques

More generally, the consequence of these special features of the Commission is that in the first decades of the Community relatively little attention was given to the institution's techniques of management. The main force for motivation has always been seen as the construction of the Community. This of course must remain the central motivating factor of a Community official. But it must not be allowed to hide the existence of real management problems for the allocation of resources as new policies develop, for the management of careers, and for the motivation of all the staff of whom only a part may feel directly involved in the construction of the European Community.

V. The Commission's staff

Who are the men and women who undertake these tasks in the Commission's services?

By total

The total number of Commission officials and temporary agents is about 16 300.

This total can be divided by function, with about 10 000 being concerned with policy and executive tasks, about 3 200 with scientific research, 2 700 with language work and 400 working in the Publications Office.

Comparisons with other organizations are difficult, because it is not easy to find any with comparable responsibilities or staff composition. In terms of total staff only, the Commission's policy and executive services are about the same size as the French Ministry of Culture or the Lord Chancellor's Department in the British Civil Service, and smaller than the total staff of the City of Amsterdam or the Comunidad Autónoma of Madrid.

Another comparison is the total cost of personnel and administration within the budget. In the Commission budget, these costs represent only some 3% of total expenditure.

One consequence of the Commission's size and specialization is also worth noting. It is torn between centralization and decentralization in its management. Some aspects of management (e.g. promotion possibilities, resource allocation) have to remain centralized because decentralized decisions would produce too much unevenness and perhaps waste. On the other hand, the specialized nature of the organization complicates the central decisions that are needed.

By source of recruitment

Every year, the Commission recruits on average some 550 officials — 150 for the A category, 100 for the LA category, 75 for the B category, 200 for the C category and 20 for the D category. These are selected from among the successful candidates in competitions which the institution organizes (sometimes together with other institutions).

The main competitions are for candidates for the starting grades in the different categories. These are organized for the different specializations that the Commission needs in its services. The Commission mainly looks for candidates who have already found a job and who are gaining work experience, so bringing with them a greater degree of expertise. And such people are acquiring the maturity to enable them to make the important career choice to take up a job abroad, with all that this implies.

The requirement that candidates should have a specialized qualification or perhaps experience reflects the fact that, with only a limited A staff, the Commission has to tackle a very wide range of tasks which often require expertise. Although general administrators are needed, so are lawyers and economists, and specialist staff such as doctors, veterinarians, minerologists, accountants and nuclear inspectors.

Because competitions are open to candidates from all the Member States, for one of the main competitions there may be as many as 10 000 applicants. These have to be sifted by written and then oral tests, after a first check of the eligibility of their application. With 12 different nationalities and educational systems to take into account, and with exams to organize in nine languages and often in 12 countries, such competitions are complicated to manage, and inevitably take many months between launching and conclusion. In the past, they have sometimes taken over two years, but the commitment has been taken to reduce the time to within 12 months.

Competition for assistants (B5) 1987	11 600 candidates
Competition for messengers (D3) 1987	5 300 candidates
Competition for administrators (A8/7) 1988	12 500 candidates
Competition for typists (C/5) 1988 (Dutch language)	2 000 candidates

It follows from this inevitably long period that the Commission cannot offer any candidate immediate employment. This is certainly a constraint, compared to the practice of some national administrations. But it has compensations.

Officials are recruited by means of competitions. Some competitions have as many as 10 000 candidates. The Commission recruits an average of some 500 new officials per year. The photo shows some of the candidates taking a written examination in such a competition.

In addition to these general competitions, the Commission also organizes a number of more specialized competitions for very specific needs, to recruit individuals or small groups of experts.

In general, the majority of our candidates come from the private sector, although the share from the public sector is highest in the A category.

By category and grade

Officials are recruited to one of the different categories, and normally to one of the starting grades. The present composition of the Commission's staff by category and grade is as follows:

On the operating budget, about 3 500 category A officials work to instructions from the Commission, preparing policies, drafting reports and legislation and supervising the execution of such legislation. This category includes all senior officials, from assistant administrators to directors-general. 1 620 LA staff are engaged in language work as either translators or interpreters. About 2 400 B officials are engaged in executive duties.

C and D officials (respectively about 4 100 and 800) are support staff. The Cs are mainly secretarial or clerical staff, while the Ds are engaged in manual or service duties.

On the research budget, the tasks undertaken at the different levels are of course different, with management and research direction undertaken at A level, and execution and support provided at the B and C levels.

An official, once recruited and after passing a probationary period, can expect to move forward through his or her category during a normal career. In the case of an A official, this means moving to A4. For B, C and D officials it means moving up to B1, C1 and D1 respectively. Movement beyond the category for B, C and D staff, and beyond A4 for A staff, is beyond the normal career, although it often happens. About 20% of intake into the C and B categories is by internal movement from the categories below, and the share is still significant, if lower, for intake into the A category. Within the A category, all but a small part of A3 staff are drawn from internal promotion, and a large share of movement to A2 and A1 also come from within, although at these levels there is more outside recruitment.

One characteristic of the Commission's services is the extent to which the separation of grade and function exists. In practice, within the grades A8 to A4, responsibility has no necessary link with the grade, although of course the more experienced and senior officials tend to be given the more important tasks. The same is true within the B category, and indeed for secretarial tasks from C5 to B2. It is only at the most senior levels, where management responsibility is specifically allocated, that a link with grade becomes essential. And even here, the management of a unit may in effect be undertaken by an A5, A4 or A3 or even an A2 official. This flexibility has developed with the Commission over the years (it is not so developed in the other institutions) as one response to the pressures on its organization.

During a career with the Commission, mobility between jobs is normal. The scope for some very specialized staff to change sectors is limited, of course, but in general, staff are encouraged to move between areas of work, at least within a directorate-general and often between services. Overall, some 12% of A staff move jobs each year.

The Jean Monnet building at the European Centre in Luxembourg, which houses the Commission's services in Luxembourg.

By status as permanent or temporary

The great majority of Commission staff on the operating budget are permanent officials, for the reasons given above.

The temporary posts that exist on the operating budget are intended to enable the Commission to recruit for strictly limited periods those with special expertise who are able to help it to carry out its tasks. In particular, the Commission makes use of these temporary posts to recruit a certain number of officials from national, regional and local administrations not only because of the expertise they can bring but in order to increase the links between the different levels of public administration in the Community.

On the research budget, on the other hand, the situation is different. Some scientific staff have the status of officials. However, since 1976, all new research staff have been engaged on fixed-term temporary contracts. These are for fixed terms for A and B staff, although

Commission departments in the Member States of

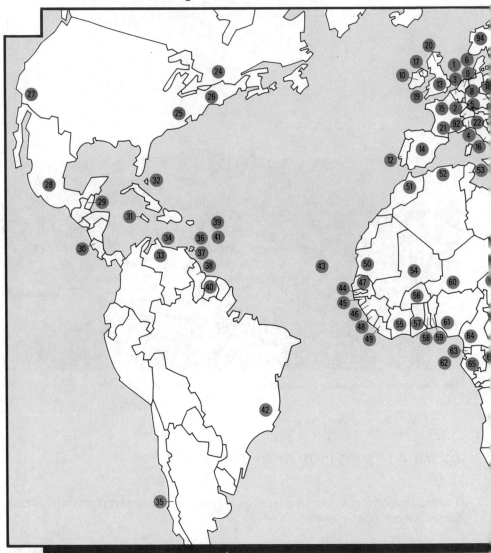

1. Brussels Belgium	A + C	
2. Luxembourg Luxembourg	A + C	
3. Geel Belgium	B	
4. Ispra Italy	B	
5. Karlsruhe Germany	B	
6. Petten Netherlands	B	
7. Athens Greece	C	
8. Bonn Germany	C	
9. The Hague Netherlands	C	
10. Dublin Ireland	C	
11. Copenhagen Denmark	C	
12. Lisbon Portugal	C	
13. London United Kingdom	C	
14. Madrid Spain	C	
15. Paris France	C + G	
16. Rome Italy	C	
17. Belfast United Kingdom	D	
18. Berlin Germany	D	
19. Cardiff United Kingdom	D	
20. Edinburgh United Kingdom	D	
21. Marseilles France	D	
22. Milan Italy	D	
23. Munich Germany	D	
24. Ottawa Canada	E	
25. Washington United States	E	
26. New York United States	C	
27. San Francisco United States	E	
28. Mexico Mexico	E	
29. Belize City Belize	F	
30. San José Costa Rica	E	
31. Kingston Jamaica	E	
32. Nassau Bahamas		
33. Caracas Venezuela	E	
34. Willemstad Netherlands Antilles	E	
35. Santiago Chile	E	
36. St Georges Grenada	F	
37. Port of Spain Trinidad and Tobago	E	
38. Georgetown Guyana	E	
39. St John's Antigua and Barbuda	F	
40. Paramaribo Suriname	E	
41. Bridgetown Barbados	E	
42. Brasilia Brazil	E	
43. Praia Capeverde	E	
44. Banjul Gambia	E	
45. Bissau Guinea-Bissau	E	
46. Conakry Guinea-Conakry	E	
47. Dakar Senegal	E	
48. Freetown Sierra Leone	E	
49. Monrovia Liberia	E	
50. Nouakchot Mauritania	E	
51. Rabat Morocco	E	
52. Algiers Algeria	E	
53. Tunis Tunisia	E	
54. Bamako Mali	E	
55. Abidjan Cote d'Ivoire	E	
56. Ouagadougou Burkina Faso	E	
57. Accra Ghana	E	

ommunity and non-member countries

A Headquarters of the Commission of the European Communities (provisional headquarters pending a final decision)
B Joint Research Centre Establishment
C Office in the Community (located in the capital of a Member State)
D Office in the Community (attached to the offices located in the capital of a Member State)
E Commission delegation in a non-member country (may take the form of a delegation, a representation or an office)
F Delegation sub-office in a non-member country (attached to a delegation in an non-member country)
G Commission delegation to an international organization (Geneva, New York, Vienna, Paris)

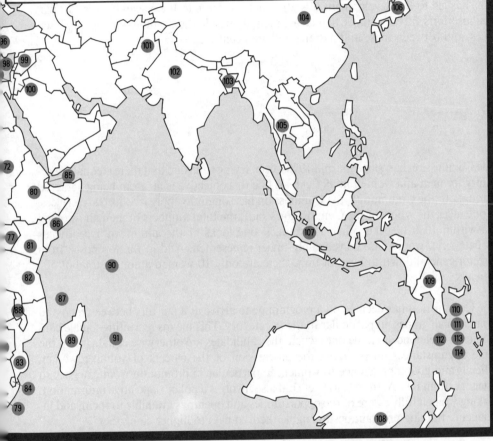

58. Lomé Togo	E	77. Kampala Uganda
59. Cotonou Benin	E	78. Harare Zimbabwe
60. Niamey Niger	E	79. Maseru Lesotho
61. Lagos Nigeria	E	80. Addis Abeba Ethiopia
62. Sao Tomé Sao Tomé and Principe	F	81. Nairobi Kenya
63. Malabo Equatorial Guinea	F	82. Dar es Salaam Tanzania
64. Yaoundé Cameroon	E	83. Maputo Mozambique
65. Libreville Gabon	E	84. Mbabane Swaziland
66. Brazzaville Congo	E	85. Djibouti Djibouti
67. Luanda Angola	E	86. Mogadishu Somalia
68. N'Djamena Chad	E	87. Moroni Comoros
69. Bangui Central African Republic	E	88. Lilongwe Malawi
70. Kinshasa Zaire	E	89. Tananarive Madagascar
71. Cairo Egypt	E	90. Victoria Mahé Seychelles
72. Khartoum Sudan	E	91. Vacoas Mauritius
73. Kigali Rwanda	E	92. Geneva Switzerland
74. Bujumbura Burundi	E	93. Vienna Austria
75. Lusaka Zambia	E	94. Oslo Norway
76. Gaborone Botswana	E	95. Belgrade Yugoslavia

77. Kampala Uganda	E
78. Harare Zimbabwe	E
79. Maseru Lesotho	E
80. Addis Abeba Ethiopia	E
81. Nairobi Kenya	E
82. Dar es Salaam Tanzania	E
83. Maputo Mozambique	E
84. Mbabane Swaziland	E
85. Djibouti Djibouti	E
86. Mogadishu Somalia	E
87. Moroni Comoros	E
88. Lilongwe Malawi	E
89. Tananarive Madagascar	E
90. Victoria Mahé Seychelles	F
91. Vacoas Mauritius	E
92. Geneva Switzerland	G
93. Vienna Austria	E + G
94. Oslo Norway	E
95. Belgrade Yugoslavia	E

96. Ankara Turkey	E
97. Tel Aviv Israel	E
98. Beirut Lebanon	E
99. Damascus Syria	E
100. Amman Jordan	E
101. Islamabad Pakistan	E
102. New Delhi India	E
103. Dhaka Bangladesh	E
104. Beijing Peoples' Republic of China	E
105. Bangkok Thailand	E
106. Tokyo Japan	E
107. Djakarta Indonesia	E
108. Canberra Australia	E
109. Boroko-Port Moresby Papua New Guinea	E
110. Honiara Solomon Islands	E
111. Apia Western Samoa	F
112. Port-Vila Vanuatu	F
113. Suva Fiji	E
114. Nuku'Alofa Tonga	F

contracts may be renewed; on second renewal they are automatically converted into contracts of indefinite duration; for other grades the contracts are for unlimited periods. A new scheme of three-year non-renewable contracts for some posts is now being introduced, to encourage mobility and interchange with other research and similar institutions.

This has led to the development of staff policies specific to the research sector. In particular, efforts are being made to increase mobility within the Commission's research services, and between these and national research centres.

By sex

The Commission has, since the mid-1970s, been trying to ensure that there is equal opportunity for men and women in all fields. While this objective is far from being achieved throughout the Community, the Commission has sought to apply it to its own services. If one takes the whole of the Commission's staff, the total numbers of men and women are within 10% of each other. However, if one looks at the administrative officials (A category), women are considerably under-represented. And in the top posts, from director-general down to head of unit, there are only 10 women among a total of 501 officials.

The Commission has decided on a programme to arrive at a fair mix between men and women in all grades, in particular in the A category. This means recruiting female candidates in preference to male ones where the candidates are otherwise equal, and in the same circumstances encouraging the progression of the careers of younger women officials and giving preference to women, in particular in promotion from category to category (from B to A, from C to B, etc.). It also involves a policy of positive information, making women fully aware of the opportunities and openings available to them, and introducing training programmes to enable them to pass to higher categories.

To help forward the policy of equality of opportunity, since 1982 a special committee has existed, made up of representatives of the administrative services most concerned and of the staff. This committee is responsible for analysing the factual situation (a study with outside experts was undertaken in 1986), for making any recommendations it thinks appropriate, and for supervising the implementation of policy.

The immediate target is to increase the proportion of women in the A category to about a quarter by 1990. All the Commission's services have been instructed to cooperate in the realization of this objective.

By nationality

The Commission's recruitment is open to the nationals of all the Member States, in accordance with the legal rules of the Community. The Commission attaches importance to achieving a balanced representation of the different nationalities in its services, in particular in the higher grades.

This is because it is important that the Commission should understand the situation in each of the Member States, and should be open to contact with them in every area of policy.

The balance of nationalities present in the Commission's services is normally achieved through the normal processes of recruitment — the competitions open to candidates from every Member State, leading to recruitment in the starting grades of each category. When an enlargement occurs, however, special arrangements are needed to enable recruitment of nationals of the new Member States at all levels of the services. These special arrangements, which last only for a limited period, have on each occasion been accompanied by arrangements for the voluntary early retirement of existing officials to make place for the new Member State nationals. In this way, it has not been necessary to create additional posts for all the recruitments made, although some new posts have been created because enlargement to include additional countries of course increases the workload of the Community.

Over the three-year period 1986-88, the Commission recruited 1 320 Spanish and Portuguese officials, who were selected as a result of 106 competitions. To make these recruitments possible, about 446 officials chose to take early retirement, while an extra 939 posts were created reflecting the fact that with enlargement comes additional work (not least because of the addition of two more languages).

The fact that the vast majority of Commission staff work away from their home country makes it necessary to provide special facilities to help new staff settle in the country to which they are posted, to help with their children's schooling and to help them with any particular difficulties they encounter during their Commission career.

In the three principal places of work of the European Commission (Brussels, Luxembourg and Ispra) Welcome offices have been established to help new officials, officials transferred from other places of work and temporary staff find out their rights and allowances, to settle in and to help and advise them about local customs and procedures.

European Schools have been established not only in the three principal places of work, but also near other Community research centres to ensure that officials' children can receive a good education in their mother tongue in the country to which the official is posted, either free or at nominal cost. The European school-leaving certificate or *baccalauréat* is now accepted by all European universities as an entrance qualification of the same level as national school-leaving certificates. And in the main centres, welfare services provide facilities for officials (e.g. nurseries for small children) and in addition offer the special advice or help that expatriate officials sometimes need.

By attitudes to work

The staff of the Commission are highly motivated by their role in the construction of the Community. They are aware of the Commission's overall objectives, believe that their work is useful and that they are called on to assume significant responsibilities. They like their working environment, relations with superiors and colleagues, and the confidence which is placed in them.

At the same time, they are critical of some aspects of their life. They find internal procedures long and complicated, they would like their individual work objectives to be more clearly defined, and they believe that the promotion system is not sufficiently open and merit-orientated.

These comments are based on two separate appreciations from the outside of the attitudes of its staff — one based on a written survey of all staff, one resulting from contact with all officials through a special management training programme — which produced surprisingly convergent results. Both were made in 1988.

The administration is now working on how to improve the weaknesses which have been revealed. This is dealt with in a later chapter.

The point to stress here is that morale is closely linked to the success of the Community. The enthusiasm that follows a further political advance for the Community can be felt in the offices and corridors and affects staff of all levels; the consequences of a failure to decide on an important issue also can be seen on the face of each official.

VI. Modernization — Response to changing conditions

Constraints

National administrations and the Commission have different tasks and working methods. This may well require different management solutions at Community and national levels. But the working environment of all public administrative systems is more similar than dissimilar.

Both at Community and at national levels there is commitment to public service. At both levels too, respect for political authority and public accountability are required.

In addition to these permanent factors, recent years have seen the impact of three particular constraints.

(i) Work allocation

First, there are fundamental changes in the societies of each of the Member States. There are several indicators of this. One is the change in university education, with a substantial increase in the numbers passing to this level of education in the last two decades. Another concerns a much greater degree of social mobility over the same period. Authority is no longer accepted without question — a factor which has to be taken into account in the way in which all organizations, whether in the public or private sectors, manage their internal structures and work. People who are now working at the Commission expect to work in a different way from how people worked when the Commission was first set up. The Commission's working methods need to evolve to take account of this situation.

(ii) New technologies

The second and perhaps more visible factor concerns the development of new technologies. No administration can today avoid using informatics, which can handle a mass of information and management procedures more quickly and more efficiently than other methods. The days are past when the introduction of a computer system necessarily imposed the rationalization of an activity; computer systems have become so flexible nowadays that they can adapt even to illogical and complex structures. Informatics opens up the prospect of more complete awareness of data, and it should provide the ability to deflect attention from processing information towards dealing with individuals.

41

(iii) Budget austerity

Thirdly, there is the tight budget climate which is common to almost all Member States. As their economies adapt to the new world structure, restrictions on the size of the public sector are being found in most countries, expressed either as a limit on growth or a freeze or even a standstill. These restrictions usually concentrate on staff numbers, because it is an easy indicator to identify.

The Community institutions in general, and the Commission in particular, have also been affected by this attitude although the expansion in Community activity has been given some recognition, and because successive enlargements have imposed the need for growth. The Commission now receives fewer new resources than it used to in the past. This is no doubt a trend that will continue and sharpen in the coming years. The Commission must therefore find a way of increasing the efficiency of all the resources at its disposal.

The Commission's response: Modernization

These constraints and pressures are nothing new for the Commission. Its services have gradually been adapting to them for years. However, in 1986 the Commission decided on a major effort to face them and update itself as necessary.

The modernization drive has concentrated on five areas: management techniques, staff policy, resource management, working procedures and informatics.

(i) Management techniques

The exercise of management responsibility is something which cannot be changed by central decision or legislation. It is reflected in the behaviour of each individual throughout the organization, at whatever level of responsibility. The Commission, like all other organizations, has many good managers and many well-run services. However, there is room for improvement. To do this, central action has been aimed at creating a climate in which all individuals feel drawn into improved management methods.

The Commisson is giving much more effort to management training. Senior officials have taken part in seminars to increase awareness of the possibilities and advantages of modern management techniques. Grouped by directorates-general, all officials, irrespective of their grade and job, have attended a seminar to make them aware of the need to improve work organization and interpersonal relations, and to suggest ways and methods of doing this.

It is apparent that there are already benefits from these training efforts. Some directors-general have launched initiatives for management methods within their own services which are producing results. Others have tightened up existing practice.

The phases of the Commission's modernization programme:

1st — Reach top management (specific seminars) — 1986, 1987.

2nd —Reach everybody (two-day seminars for whole DGs, questionnaire) — 1988.

3rd — Assessment by each DG of what had been learnt — 1988, 1989.

4th — Central support for local action in each DG according to its needs — 1989, 1990.

5th — To be defined — 1990+.

(ii) Staff management

In parallel with the effort to improve management techniques, the Commission is seeking to improve the quality of staff management. This is an area which is the primary responsibility of each director-general and his hierarchy. It is not possible, nor desirable, to organize centrally the main elements of each individual's career: the content of his or her work, career planning, mobility, training and promotion prospects. However, the Commission has taken a certain number of measures centrally to contribute towards improved staff policy.

Recruitment procedures have been reviewed and improvements introduced to speed up the recruitment process, particularly for the main recruiting competitions to the starting grades of each category. Our aim is to hold competitions in the main sectors of recruitment at regular, pre-announced intervals, and to complete the competitions within 12 months. An improved method of training new recruits has also been introduced.

Likewise, training for staff in mid-career has been considerably developed. Language training, obviously an important activity in the multilingual and multicultural environment that exists at the Commission, has been reorganized and extended to give priority above all to training required in the interests of the service. Further development is in prospect. Training to help officials develop their careers has also been extended. And, of course, informatics training has grown very rapidly.

Another aspect of career development that has grown substantially have been contacts and exchanges with national administrations. Commission officials participate in training courses offered by national civil service training organizations. The system of exchanges which exists between officials of the Commission and of national administra-

43

tions is now being extended so that Commission officials go for some months to a Member State other than their own for basic language training and to have contact with the culture and political context of the country concerned. This will remain a form of training but will be very valuable in helping to reinforce the Community awareness of Commission officials.

(iii) Resource management

Over the last years the Commission has developed management instruments to enable it to find staff and other resources from within to meet changing policy needs. At the same time it has sought to use to best effect all the possibilities available within the budget and to make absolutely clear through the budget how it uses its resources.

The main mechanism that has been developed to this end is a five-year rolling programme for the use of staff resources. This is a complicated instrument that was at first resisted as being unnecessary by the services. However, it has taken some years to develop and it is now largely accepted as useful not only for central allocation of resources but also within each directorate-general.

Helped by the rolling programme, there is an annual allocation of staff resources in accordance with needs across the Commission's services. The Commission is thus able to meet its most pressing priorities.

The resources allocated come from different sources. These can be from within the directorate-general, with posts transferred from another activity. They can be from a central reserve of posts, created by pooling a small percentage every year of the established staff of all services. They might be new posts which the budget authority has agreed in the annual budget. Or they might be resources from outside the Commission, such as study contracts or consultants to whom work is farmed out, or national officials who are brought in to supplement the Commission's staff under the exchange scheme.

The Commission has also set itself the objective of redeploying 7.5% of its policy staff towards new and priority tasks by the end of 1990.

(iv) Simplification of procedures

Another source of modernization, and of gaining resources, is to reduce the complexity of internal procedures. These not only take time but may also reduce individual responsibility or initiative. Procedures in some areas have already been reviewed. These areas are financial delegation, contracting procedures and responsibility for concluding external studies.

Two principles have guided the Commission in carrying out these reviews. One has been to increase decentralization so that individual directors-general and their services take financial responsibility for activities for which they bear the policy responsibility.

The second has been to encourage delegation from the level of director-general to lower levels in each service. It is important that the exercise of decentralization and delegation should not lead to lack of control. However, there is certainly scope in the Commission for going further in these directions before there is any risk of loss of control.

(v) Informatics

The principle of decentralization of responsibility has also been applied for some years in the field of informatics. Each directorate-general draws up a plan for developing its use of informatics. The central informatics service provides certain large-scale computer facilities, guidance, training, equipment and software. This principle of 'user-driven' development of informatics has led to some unevenness in the degree to which different services use the new technologies. But as time goes by these unevennesses are being reduced. By the end of the decade one official in two will have direct access to a terminal.

At end-1988, there were nearly 6 000 work stations in the Commission services, the result of growth at a rate of 30% in recent years (from 2 640 in 1984). By 1990, the number will have risen to 8 300. Overall, the informatics capacity available will increase over the same period from 480 mips to 950 mips.

As part of its approach the Commission has insisted that the development of new technology within each directorate-general forms part of an overall strategy. All equipment is compatible and will be linked to the Commission network so that it can all intercommunicate.

An electronic mail system capable of communication between all the different types and makes of equipment used by its services has been developed by the Commission. It can thus work with equipment from different manufacturers. This enables the Commission to choose the most cost-efficient items within each manufacturer's product range and to be in a strong position to negotiate with suppliers. As a result considerable budget savings have been achieved. There has also been a very substantial increase in informatics coverage throughout the Commission over the last few years with no increase to the budget in the real cost of this area of activity.

The Commission also tries to interest the national Member State administrations so that as electronic mail and message handling becomes more of a reality the different national administrations and the Community institutions will be able easily to transmit messages and papers between themselves.

The extension of informatics has enabled the Commission to review different organizational structures within its administration, and to simplify work procedures.

VII. The future: Europe versus Eurocracy?

The Community needs a unique administrative structure

The Community is a political structure unique in the world. Its legal and institutional framework is unlike that of any other grouping. It requires an administration which corresponds to its ambition. But this makes it necessary to find administrative structures which match the needs of a population of more than 320 million people spread over more than 2.25 million square kilometres. This cannot be done by concentrating administration in Brussels and Luxembourg, thousands of kilometres from many of the governments, the citizens and the industries concerned. The need to develop a unique administration is even more necessary as the Community develops towards 1992 and beyond.

This was recognized at the outset of the Community, and has been further developed since then.

Community activity is often administered by national public services

The Treaties provide that one of the main instruments for the Community to implement its decisions is by way of directives, which lay upon the Member States, who have all been parties to their decision, the obligation to implement their content through national legislation, if necessary by new or amended laws. Thus implementation is a matter for national administrations, and if necessary the national courts (which may refer matters to the Court of Justice in Luxembourg for interpretation). The Commission's task is only to ensure that national law does indeed correspond to the decisions that have been taken at Community level. Most of the decisions that the Community takes in the area of industry are of this type.

Other and different examples can be found of involvement of national administrations in Community affairs. The two most important are customs and agriculture. Customs duties are decided by the Community, and their proceeds belong directly to the Community, being part of the Community's 'own resources'. They are, however, collected and administered by the customs services of the different Member States, with the help of some central coordination on common problems from the appropriate Commission service. The common agricultural policy, which directly affects the daily activity of farmers

47

throughout the Community, is not administered only by the 800 or so officials in the Commission in Brussels who could not possibly keep in touch with 10 million people working in agriculture. The decisions are made in Brussels through the Community's decision-making machinery. But the day-to-day administration is carried out by many thousands of officials in the different agricultural ministries around the Community at national and sometimes regional level.

It is true that the Commission administers directly some areas which may have a direct impact on firms and even the citizen. Examples are in certain areas of nuclear safety, veterinary standards and fisheries. The Commission finances projects in many areas by firms as well as by public sector organizations, sometimes but not always put forward by the Member States. In the field of competition policy, it can and does control the respect of Community anti-trust law and decides fines which companies have to pay.

In addition, in some areas, limited at present, the Commission entrusts tasks to private or semi-private sector bodies.

But the bulk of Community activity is administered not by officials in Brussels but through national and regional administrations.

The Commission remains small

The result is that the Commission remains a very small organization in relation to its responsibilities for the development, management and control of Community policies affecting all the Member States.

This smallness, and the close links with national and regional administrations, is a source of strength for the Community. It means that administration is close to those affected, that discussion and explanation can be held in almost all cases without having to have recourse to Brussels or Luxembourg and to administrative structures which are little known or understood.

There is no 'vast Brussels bureaucracy' which takes decisions in ignorance of the situations of the individual region, firm or citizen. The main decisions are taken by democratically chosen ministers of national governments meeting in the Council, with the help of the Parliament elected through universal suffrage. And there is an enormous amount of contact with the Member States in the administering of policies.

1992 is a challenge for the Community's administrative structure

It is important that this situation should continue in the future. The Community has been set by the Member States on a path of even greater ambition, by the signature and·

ratification of the Single Act in 1986. This commits the Community to achieving by 1992 the completion of the internal market and the development over the same period of important accompanying policies (involving a virtual doubling of the structural Funds). The Act also provides a new basis for common action in the fields of social affairs, environment and research, and provides for further development towards economic and monetary cohesion. At the same time, the Community is developing in many other areas, including agricultural, commercial and development policy, telecommunications, employment and education.

Continue to rely on national and regional public services

This activity has been decided at political level. But it requires administration to turn political will into reality. Can this be achieved by the same methods as in the past, relying heavily on national administrations?

The Commission hopes so. It believes that the institutional balance of power laid down in the Treaties should be maintained. This is necessary for Community policies to develop correctly in the future. But it is clear that decentralization of management within frameworks decided and maintained in accordance with Community procedures, and subject to the control of Community bodies concerned (especially the Parliament and the Court of Auditors) is needed to help the Community reach all parts of the Member States.

Indeed this is part of a process which is much broader than the Community institutions. In almost every Member State there is currently a move to decentralize and delegate responsibilities from the central administration to other bodies, often at regional level. The Community should be part of this overall process.

The future growth of the central administration should be limited

The Commission may nevertheless grow further in the future. As the tasks of the Community grow in accordance with the will of the Member States (including some responsibilities transferred to the Community), so some additional responsibilities will inevitably have to be undertaken at the centre. But the Commission wants this growth to be limited, and to see increased Community activity reflected in additional resources elsewhere than in its central services.

Develop Community agencies to take on specific tasks

In addition to the increasing tasks to be undertaken by the Member States at national and regional levels, the Commission is examining the scope for entrusting some of its specific management activities to agencies. The sort of tasks in question would be specific and within well-defined policy parameters; they would also often require specialist staff. Such agencies could well be geographically dispersed in the Community.

Management improvement remains essential

This makes the modernization programme essential, as it is the way in which existing officials become increasingly able to adapt to changing tasks as the political horizons of the Community develop and the methods of management evolve.

Strengthen links between Community, national and regional administrations

As part of the strategy it is very important that the Commission further develops its links with the national and regional administrations. This is why it has recently sought an increase in the number of temporary posts, so that more people can come and work in the institution for a strictly limited period, and then return to the national level — whether in the public or private sector — with first-hand knowledge of how the Community works. The scheme by which national or regional officials come to the Commission for periods of up to three years while remaining in their existing employment has also been developed to build up the number of those in these layers of administration who have experience of working of the Community.

In addition, there are plans to send Commission officials more systematically for training to different Member States other than their own to give them some knowledge of the political and administrative structures at central and regional levels and of the language of the country. This will be valuable to increase further the Community spirit of our officials, as well as helping to develop contacts between the different layers of administration.

In the context of increasing links between the different levels of administration, the way in which public services develop in the Member States and at Community level is a further dimension of this many-sided strategy. Of course each country has different traditions, needs, and structures. But it is helpful for each public service to be aware of the way in which the others in the Community are confronting the new situations in which they are placed, so that where there are parallels the broad trends of development may be in harmony. For this reason, there are regular if well-spaced meetings between the heads of the different public services.

The Commission and the Member States are also concerned about the way in which the national and regional administrations need to evolve as their involvement in the Community increases. In this context, training is one important element, and contacts with the national administrations are developing to identify training needs in Community affairs for national and regional efforts and to see how best to meet them, with the help of existing organizations at Community level.

The aim: Avoid Eurocracy

In all these ways, the Commission remains determined that the development of the Community should not be accompanied by a parallel growth in a central bureaucracy. We are in practice forging a new model of public administration to match the uniqueness of the Community. The task of carrying this forward into the future is a challenge that is worth while.

Basic posts in the staff structure of the Commission

This is a simplified table, giving only administrative posts and not those for the language, technical or research staff (which, however, follow the same grading structure, with different descriptions for the different levels).

Category A

Director-general (or deputy director-general)	A1
Director (or principal adviser)	A2
Head of unit (or adviser)	A3, A4 or A5
Principal administrator	A4 or A5
(or head of section, deputy head of unit)	
Administrator	A6 or A7
Assistant administrator	A8

Category B

Principal administrative assistant (head of office)	B1
Senior administrative assistant	B2 or B3
Administrative assistant	B4 or B5

Category C

Executive or principal secretary, principal clerical officer	C1
Secretary/shorthand typist, clerical officer	C2 or C3
Typist, clerical assistant	C4 or C5

Category D

Head of group	D1
Skilled employee	D2 or D3
Unskilled employee	D4

Salaries of Community officials and temporary agents

As of 1.1.1989 basic monthly salaries are determined for each grade and step as provided for in the following table (amounts in Belgian francs):

Grades	Steps							
	1	2	3	4	5	6	7	8
A 1	338 457	356 438	374 419	392 400	410 381	428 362		
A 2	300 358	317 515	334 672	351 829	368 986	386 143		
A 3 / LA 3	248 755	263 761	278 767	293 773	308 779	323 785	338 791	353 797
A 4 / LA 4	208 977	220 690	232 403	244 116	255 829	267 542	279 255	290 968
A 5 / LA 5	172 292	182 499	192 706	202 913	213 120	223 327	233 534	243 741
A 6 / LA 6	148 889	157 013	165 137	173 261	181 385	189 509	197 633	205 757
A 7 / LA 7	128 161	134 539	140 917	147 295	153 673	160 051		
A 8 / LA 8	113 351	117 920						
B 1	148 889	157 013	165 137	173 261	181 385	189 509	197 633	205 757
B 2	129 005	135 052	141 099	147 146	153 193	159 240	165 287	171 334
B 3	108 204	113 234	118 264	123 294	128 324	133 354	138 384	143 414
B 4	93 589	97 950	102 311	106 672	111 033	115 394	119 755	124 116
B 5	83 655	87 186	90 717	94 248				
C 1	95 459	99 307	103 155	107 003	110 851	114 699	118 547	122 395
C 2	83 027	86 555	90 083	93 611	97 139	100 667	104 195	107 723
C 3	77 451	80 473	83 495	86 517	89 539	92 561	95 583	98 605
C 4	69 978	72 814	75 650	78 486	81 322	84 158	86 994	89 830
C 5	64 533	67 175	69 817	72 459				
D 1	72 927	76 115	79 303	82 491	85 679	88 867	92 055	95 243
D 2	66 494	69 325	72 156	74 987	77 818	80 649	83 480	86 311
D 3	61 890	64 538	67 186	69 834	72 482	75 130	77 778	80 426
D 4	58 353	60 746	63 139	65 532				

Family allowances

Household allowance, fixed at 5% of the basic salary or BFR 4 954 whichever is the greater.

Dependent child allowance is BFR 6 381 per month for each dependent child.

Education allowance, equal to the *actual* education costs incurred and up to a maximum of BFR 5 701.

Expatriation allowance

Expatriation allowance, equal to 16% of the total amount of the basic salary plus household allowance and the dependent child allowance or BFR 11 397 whichever is the greater, is paid to staff who were recruited from a country other than their place of work.

Deductions

Salaries are subject to a progressive Community tax for which the maximum rate is 45%, on a scale as follows, with effect from 1 July 1988:

```
8    % to amounts between BFR     2 561 and  45 211
10   % to amounts between BFR   45 212 and  62 271
10.5 % to amounts between BFR   62 272 and  71 366
15   % to amounts between BFR   71 367 and  81 037
17.5 % to amounts between BFR   81 038 and  90 132
20   % to amounts between BFR   90 133 and  98 949
22.5 % to amounts between BFR   98 950 and 108 047
25   % to amounts between BFR  108 048 and 116 864
27.5 % to amounts between BFR  116 865 and 125 958
30   % to amounts between BFR  125 959 and 134 775
32.5 % to amounts between BFR  134 776 and 143 873
35   % to amounts between BFR  143 874 and 152 690
40   % to amounts between BFR  152 691 and 161 785
45   % to amounts above     BFR 161 785
```

A crisis levy (currently of 7.62 %) is also imposed. This rate is applied to that part of the salary representing the difference between the net salary of an official receiving no allowances and an amount equal to the basic salary of a D4-1.

Pension contributions are 6.75 % of basic salary.

Sickness and accident insurance contributions are 1.45 % of basic salaray.

Staff numbers: Maximum authorized staff (budget 1989)

1. Total by institution

Parliament	3 405
Council	2 165
Economic and Social Committee	494
Commission	16 309
Court of Justice	682
Court of Auditors	377
Total	**23 432**

2. Commission by organization

Operational departments	9 911
Research staff	3 176
Language staff (estimated - see page 21)	2 700
Total	**15 787**

Publications Office	406
Centre for the Development of Vocational Training	61
Foundation for the Improvement of Living and Working Conditions (Dublin)	55
Total	**16 309**

3. Commission by category and grade (permanent and temporary)

	Operating	Research	Total
A1	26	2	28
A2	159	22	181
A3	439	98	537
A4	906	373	1 279
A5	807	379	1 186
A6	607	211	818
A7	546	107	653
A8	16	15	31
Total	**3 506**	**1 207**	**4 713**

	Operating	Research	Total
LA3	31		
LA4	308		
LA5	524		
LA6	342		
LA7	414		
LA8	1		
Total	1 620	....	1 620
B1	617	215	832
B2	568	289	857
B3	647	223	870
B4	421	163	584
B5	334	72	406
Total	2 587	962	3 549
C1	926	426	1 352
C2	897	338	1 235
C3	1 279	116	1 395
C4	538	60	598
C5	449	28	477
Total	4 089	968	5 057
D1	269	36	305
D2	209	3	212
D3	331	—	331
D4	—	—	—
Total	809	39	848
Grand total	12 611	3 176	15 787

Number of staff employed by the Commission (1.1.1989)

1. Total

	Operating	Research	Total
A	3 402	875	4 277
LA	1 528	—	1 528
B	2 489	761	3 250
C	4 189	866	5 055
D	782	46	828
Total	12 390	2 548	14 938

2. By status, permanent/temporary

	Operating		Research		Total	
	Perm.	Temp.	Perm.	Temp.	Perm.	Temp.
A	3 221	181	458	417	3 679	598
LA	1 314	214	—	—	1 314	214
B	2 422	67	544	217	2 966	284
C	4 043	146	119	747	4 162	893
D	743	39	2	44	745	83
Total	11 743	647	1 123	1 425	12 866	2 072

3. By sex (%)

	Operating		Research		Total	
	M	F	M	F	M	F
A ...	89 ...	11	94 ...	6	90 ...	10
LA ..	50 ...	50	— ...	—	50 ...	50
B	63 ...	37	87 ...	13	69 ...	10
C	21 ...	79	61 ...	39	28 ...	72
D ...	75 ...	25	74 ...	26	75 ...	25
Total .	55 ...	45	80 ...	20	59 ...	41

4. By nationality (operating and research budgets combined)

	B	DK	D	GR	E	F	IRL	I	L	NL	P	UK	other	Total
A ..	539	103	686	183	353	673	125	652	66	234	154	494	15	4 277
LA .	171	131	204	129	165	114	15	184	7	87	107	192	22	1 528
B ..	834	61	416	86	229	389	73	545	99	230	78	198	12	3 250
C ..	1 691	134	484	140	232	415	105	1 069	244	161	126	238	16	5 055
D ..	286	6	16	26	14	57	1	310	71	9	16	10	6	828
Total	3 521	435	1 806	564	993	1 648	319	2 760	487	721	481	1 132	71	14 938

5. By age (operating budget, officials and temporary agents — %)

	30	31-35	36-40	41-45	46-50	51-55	56-60	61-65
A	4	11	19	18	15	16	12	5
LA	14	16	23	20	11	8	4	4
B	6	16	20	14	14	15	9	5
C	15	20	21	18	12	8	4	2
D	13	20	18	19	12	10	6	2
Total ...	10	16	20	18	14	12	6	4

6. By DG

Cabinets			294
Secretariat-General			335
Legal Service			170
Spokesman's Service			52
Consumer Policy Service			40
Task Force 'Human resources, education, training and youth'			55
Translation Service			1 678
Joint Interpretation and Conference Service			506
Statistical Office			352
DG	I	— External Relations	613
DG	II	— Economic and Financial Affairs	231
DG	III	— Internal Market and Industrial Affairs	430
DG	IV	— Competition	309
DG	V	— Employment, Industrial Relationships and Social Affairs	295
DG	VI	— Agriculture	826
DG	VII	— Transport	127
DG	VIII	— Development	766
DG	IX	— Personnel and Administration	2 536
DG	X	— Information, Communication and Culture	369
DG	XI	— Environment, Nuclear Safety and Civil Protection	119
DG	XII	— Science, Research and Development	501
		Joint Research Centre	1 985
DG	XIII	— Telecommunications, Information Industries and Innovation	492
DG	XIV	— Fisheries	164
DG	XV	— Financial Institutions and Company Law	82
DG	XVI	— Regional Policies	196
DG	XVII	— Energy	409
DG	XVIII	— Credit and Investments	101
DG	XIX	— Budgets	260
DG	XX	— Financial Control	164
DG	XXI	— Customs Union and Indirect Taxation	229
DG	XXII	— Coordination of Structural Policies	60
DG	XXIII	— Enterprises' Policy, Distributive Trades, Tourism and Social Economy	56
Euratom Supply Agency			23
Security Office			55

7. By place of employment

Brussels	9 854
Luxembourg	2 349
Ispra (Joint Research Centre)	1 587
Other Research Centres	528
Press and Information Offices in the Community	157
Delegations outside the Community (incl. ACP, etc.)	414
Other	49
Total	14 938

Further reading

Amerasinghe, C.F. *Law of the international civil service* (as applied by international administrative tribunals) Oxford, Clarendon 1988, 2 vol.

'Britons in Brussels, Officials in the European Commission and Council Secretariat' Virginia Willis. Royal Institute of Public Administration, London, Policy Studies Institute 1982, VI, 109 pp. *Studies in European Politics*

Conrad, Yves. *Jean Monnet et les débuts de la fonction publique européenne. La Haute Autorité de la CECA (1952-1953),* Louvain-la-Neuve, Ciaco éd. 1988, 162 pp.

CEE, Voyage en Eurocratie, Bernard Brigouleix. Paris: Ed. Moreau 1986, 282 pp.

'Community bureaucracy at the crossroads — l'Administration communautaire à l'heure du choix', Colloquium organized by the College of Europe, Bruges, 21 to 23 October 1987, J. Jamar, W. Wessels, ed. Bruges, De Tempel 1985, VI, 415 pp. *Cahiers de Bruges* NS 42

L'égalité des chances à la Commission des Communautés européennes, Monique Chalude, Robin Chater, Jacqueline Laufer, EC Commission, Brussels: Chalude and Ass. 1986 (pag. diff.) (COPEC (87) 162)

La fonction publique européenne, Dieter Rogalla. Brussels (etc.), 1982, 351 pp.

'Report on the situation of women in the European institutions', EC European Parliament, Committee on Women's Rights. Rapporteur: Ien van den Heuvel. Luxembourg, *EP Documents* 1986/0257 A2

Commission of the European Communities
Rue de la Loi 200, B-1049 Bruxelles

Bureau en Belgique
Bureau in België

Rue Archimède 73
1040 Bruxelles
Archimedesstraat 73
1040 Brussel
Tél. 235 38 44
Télex 26 657 COMINF B
Télécopie 235 01 66

Kontor i Danmark

Højbrohus
Østergade 61
Postbox 144
1004 København K
Tlf.: 33 14 41 40
Telex 16 402 COMEUR DK
Telefax 33 11 12 03 / 33 14 12 44

Vertretung in der Bundesrepublik Deutschland

Zitelmannstraße 22
5300 Bonn
Tel. 53 00 90
Fernschreiber 886 648 EUROP D
Fernkopie 5 30 09 50

Außenstelle Berlin
Kurfürstendamm 102
1000 Berlin 31
Tel.: 8 92 40 28
Fernschreiber 184 015 EUROP D
Fernkopie 8 92 20 59

Vertretung in München
Erhardstraße 27
8000 München 2
Tel.: 2 02 10 11
Fernschreiber 5 218 135
Fernkopie 2 02 10 15

Γραφείο στην Ελλάδα

2, Vassilissis Sofias
T.K. 11 002
106 74 Athina
Tel. 724 39 82/3/4
Telex 219 324 ECAT GR
Telefax 724 46 20

Oficina en España

Calle de Serrano 41, 5ª
28001 Madrid
Tel. 435 17 00 / 435 15 28
Télex 46 818 OIPE
Telecopia 276 03 87

Bureaux de représentation en France
Bureau à Paris

61, rue des Belles-Feuilles
75782 Paris Cedex 16
Tél. 45 01 58 85
Télex Paris 611 019 COMEUR
Télécopie 47 27 26 07

Bureau à Marseille
CMCI
2, rue Henri-Barbusse
13241 Marseille Cedex 01
Tél. 91 91 46 00
Télex 402 538 EURMA
Télécopie 91 90 98 07

Office in Ireland

39, Molesworth Street
Dublin 2
Tel. 71 22 44
Telex 93 827 EUCO EI
Telefax 71 26 57

Ufficio in Italia

Via Poli, 29
00187 Roma
Tel. 678 97 22
Telex 610 184 EUROMA I
Telecopia 679 16 58

Ufficio a Milano
Corso Magenta, 59
20123 Milano
Tel. 80 15 05
Telex 316 200 EURMIL I
Telecopia 481 85 43

Bureau au Luxembourg

Bâtiment Jean Monnet B/O
2920 Luxembourg
Tél. 430 11
Télex 3423/3446 COMEUR LU
Télécopie 43 01 44 33

Bureau in Nederland

Korte Vijverberg 5
2513 AB Den Haag
Tel. 46 93 26
Telex 31 094 EURCO NL
Telefax 64 66 19

Gabinete em Portugal

Centro Europeu Jean Monnet
Largo Jean Monnet, 1-10°
1200 Lisboa
Tel. 54 11 44
Telex 18 810 COMEUR P
Telecópia 55 43 97

Office in the United Kingdom

Jean Monnet House
8, Storey's Gate
London SW1P 3AT
Tel. 222 8122
Telex 23 208 EURUK G
Telefax 222 09 00 / 222 81 20

Office in Northern Ireland
Windsor House
9/15 Bedford Street
Belfast BT2 7EG
Tel. 240 708
Telex 74 117 CECBEL G
Telefax: 248 241

Office in Wales
4 Cathedral Road
PO Box 15
Cardiff CF1 9SG
Tel. 37 16 31
Telex 497 727 EUROPA G
Telefax 39 54 89

Office in Scotland
7 Alva Street
Edinburgh EH2 4PH
Tel. 225 20 58
Telex 727 420 EUEDIN G
Telefax 226 41 05

United States of America

Washington
2100 M Street NW
(Suite 707)
Washington, DC 20037
Tel. (202) 862 95 00
Telex 64 215 EURCOM NW
Telefax 429 17 66

New York
Suboffice to the Washington office
3, Dag Hammarskjöld Plaza
305 East 47th Street
New York, NY 10017
Tel. (212) 371 38 04
Telex 012 396 EURCOM NY
Telefax 758 27 18

Nippon

Tokyo
Europa House
9-15 Sanbancho
Chiyoda-Ku
Tokyo 102
Tel. 239 04 41
Telex 28 567 COMEUTOK J
Telefax 261 51 94

Schweiz-Suisse-Svizzera

Genève
Case postale 195
37-39, rue de Vermont
1211 Genève 20
Tél. 34 97 50
Télex 282 61/2 ECOM CH
Télécopie 34 23 31

Venezuela

Caracas
Avenida Orinoco
Las Mercedes
Apartado 67 076
Las Américas 1061 A
Caracas
Tel. 91 51 33
Télex 27-298 COMEU VC
Telecopia 91 88 76

Europe is ours.
Let's get to know it!

Maps of the European Community —
Political and thematic maps

Four maps of the Community printed in up to eight colours are now on sale at reasonable prices: a political map of the 12 Member States, their regions and main administrative units, an agricultural map showing the main lines of production for each region, a forestry map and a demographic map showing population density by region, main towns and conurbations and population trends.

All the maps measure 75 x 105 cm, scale 1:4 000 000 (1 cm = 40 km), and are available folded (25 x 13 cm) or flat in the following languages: Danish, Dutch French, English, German, Greek, Italian, Portuguese and Spanish.

The European Community — Political map

Member States, regions and administrative units

The political map shows the 12 Member States which have made up the European Community since 1 January 1986 (Belgium, Denmark, Federal Republic of Germany, Greece, Spain, France, Ireland, Italy, Luxembourg, The Netherlands, Portugal and United Kingdom), their subdivisions into regions and administrative units (provinces, counties, etc.), and capitals (national and regional) and main towns respectively.

The European Community now covers 2.25 million sq km and has a population of 320 million.

In addition to the map proper there is an inset containing 105 diagrams giving economic and other statistics on the European Community and its Member States, and comparative figures for the Soviet Union and the United States.

Forests of the European Community

This unique map shows all the woodlands of the Community right down to local level. There are 54 million hectares of woodland in the Community covering one quarter of its total area. At first sight this is reassuring, but the situation varies a great deal from one country to another.

There is an inset on the map containing a large number of diagrams giving statistics for each Member State and for the Community as a whole, together with comparisons between the Community and the other major wood producers in the world.

Printed in 1987, this map covers the 12 countries of the European Community: Belgium, Denmark, Federal Republic of Germany, Greece, Spain, France, Ireland, Italy, Luxembourg, The Netherlands, Portugal and United Kingdom.

Farming in the European Community

More than half the land area of the European Community is cultivated. For the first time the farming map shows the agricultural land of the 12 Member States.

Different colours are used to identify the less-favoured farming areas: mountain and hill areas where farming is possible but expensive; regions of low productivity where agriculture is essential to prevent still more people leaving the land; and areas with small farms with specific handicaps. The main line of production in each region is shown by means of symbols.

A large number of diagrams give statistics on agricultural production, together with detailed information on the agricultural imports and exports of each Member State and of the Community as a whole. They also give figures for the world's two other leading agricultural producers: the United States and the Soviet Union.

The population of the European Community, present and future

The Community's population is declining rapidly, a downward trend highlighted in this new population map of the European Community.

The map, of all 12 Member States, shows in fascinating detail the population density of the Community's almost 200 regions and the main towns and conurbations, which differ considerably in size from one country to another.

There is also an inset containing a large number of statistics, by country, with comparisons between the European Community, the United States and the Soviet Union. These include current population densities and projections to 2020, population by age group, birth rates, ageing, and employment and unemployment levels.

Prices in Luxembourg, excluding VAT and postage:

	ECU
Political map	5.45
Population map	7.00
Farming map	5.45
Woodlands map	5.45
Four-map set	17.40

The maps are obtainable from:

United Kingdom

Ordnance Survey
Romsey Road
Maybush
Southampton SO9 4DH

HMSO BOOKS (PC 16)
HMSO Publications Centre
51 Nine Elms Lane
London SW8 5DR
Tel. (01) 211 77 02

Sub-agent:

Alan Armstrong & Associates Ltd
Arkwright Road
Reading, Berks RG 2 0SQ
Tel. (0734) 75 17 69
Telex 849937 AAALTD G

Ireland

Ordnance Survey Office
Phoenix Park
Dublin

Government Publications Sales Office
(EEC Section)
Sun Alliance House
Molesworth Street
Dublin 2
Tel. 71 03 09

or by post

Government Stationery Office
EEC Section
6th floor
Bishop Street
Dublin 8
Tel. 78 16 66

United States of America

European Community Information Service
2100 M Street NW
Suite 707
Washington, DC 20037
Tel. (202) 862 9500

Canada

Renouf Publishing Co., Ltd
61 Sparks St (Mall)
Ottawa
Ontario K1P 5R1
Tel. Toll Free 1-800-267-4164
Ottawa Region (613) 238-8985-6

Japan

Kinokuniya Company, Ltd
17-7 Shinjuku 3-Chome
Shinjuku-ku
Tokyo 160-91
Tel. (03) 354 0131

Other countries

Office for Official Publications
of the European Communities
2, rue Mercier
L-2985 Luxembourg
Tel. 499 28-1
Telex 1324 b PUBOF LU

European Communities — Commission

The European Commission and the administration of the Community

Richard Hay, Director-General of Personnel and Administration, Commission of the European Communities

Luxembourg: Office for Official Publications of the European Communities

1989 — 63 pp. — 16.2 x 22.9 cm

European Documentation series — 1989

ES, DA, DE, GR, EN, FR, IT, NL, PT

ISBN 92-825-9907-8

Catalogue number: CB-NC-89-003-EN-C

Description of the European civil service: origins, tasks, originality and development.